a growing love

by ulrich schaffer

for the love of children
a growing love
love reaches out
searching for you

a growing love

meditations on marriage and
commitment

ulrich schaffer

*with photographs
by the author*

HARPER & ROW, PUBLISHERS

SAN FRANCISCO

Cambridge
Hagerstown
Philadelphia
New York

London
Mexico City
São Paulo
Sydney

1817

Library of Congress Cataloging in Publication Data

Schaffer, Ulrich, 1942-
   A growing love.

   Poems.
   1. Marriage—Poetry. I. Title.
PR9199.3.S26G7   1980   811w.54   79-3758
ISBN 0-06-067079-7

80 81 82 83 84 10 9 8 7 6 5 4 3 2 1

for dorothy and gordon
and
margie and steve
and
all those who are struggling with us
for an understanding
of what it can mean
to be married today

love is the only force
that can make things one
without destroying them.

—teilhard de chardin

contents

what's really happening?

thank you for . . .

about the author

three marriages

One reason why marriage seems so unacceptable to many people is the conspicuous absence of convincing, interesting marriages. When I ask young people if they know at least one marriage which they might want to use as a model for their own, there is often a silence. Marriages of Christians are little or no exception here. We lack exemplary marriages from which we can learn how to live with one another without dying in the relationship, without being killed as persons, without becoming indifferent to each other.

This book is a series of reflections on marriage, written at a time when many people think of marriage as a thing of the past. Some even feel that commitment is a weakness, an outdated virtue. Yet, is there another way to build meaningful relationships but by committing oneself to another person and to growth with that person?

It seems that almost all marriages or close relationships fall into one of the following three groups:

The first is the traditional, conservative marriage in which roles and duties are clear. Paul's writings concerning women are often quoted in these marriages, without the partners paying much attention to the context in which Paul wrote. These marriages are generally very predictable. The partners know what is expected of them and they reiterate this to each other. These marriages are "safe" and "secure" because there is not much openness about new ways of being together. There is also much death in them, much rejecting of one's own and the other's total being. There is much denying of what one feels. Often these marriages reflect a world that does not exist anymore. They are not in touch with the world as it exists now and therefore do not offer constructive suggestions on how to live in a changing world—a world of Future Shock, of Women's Liberation, of birth control, of starvation, of affluence, and of potential self-annihilation.

Instead of growth there is only repetition in these marriages.

The second kind of marriage seems, in many ways, to be the opposite of the first kind. Everything is open and allowed. Both partners give each other great "freedom" to do as they like, perhaps even considering sexual intimacy outside of marriage as part of that "freedom."

In an attempt not to make the mistakes of the first kind of marriage, of squashing the other person, the partners in this marriage die in the cold of isolation and alienation, thinly disguised as "swinging," as "being free." There are no permanent roles here but there is also no commitment. There is little concern about discovering the depths in the partner and working out the differences in a way that will benefit both.

Instead of growth in these marriages there is only indifference.

The third kind of marriage is difficult to define or grasp. There are no roles and yet there is commitment. There is freedom, but it does not lead to indifference. These marriages and relationships are breaking new ground, trying to tap the tremendous potential of a growth-partnership. They are "endangered" marriages because they are in the process of changing, of becoming. There is little "safe hiding" in roles. They are unpredictable because each partner gives the other freedom, but both are still committed to each other. These marriages are exciting to watch because they perform a sort of tightrope act between the other two alternatives. They are upheld by their faith and they can therefore dare to be pioneers.

The mark of these marriages is a close proximity of joy and pain, because in the full experience of each other there will always be joy and pain, elation and disappointment, happiness and sadness. In this marriage there is room for the full gamut of feelings. All emotions are acknowledged. Both partners take each other seriously as individuals. Both help each other to grow, to realize their full potential in every area of life.

The reflections in this book are to be understood in the light of the third kind of marriage. I am trying to touch on those areas where friction often arises and where we need to find a new way of dealing creatively with that friction. I am trying to get away from the standard responses: "Don't think that!" "That is wrong / right," "You mustn't say that." Those statements generally do not further growth and give us no new insights.

This book does not claim to be complete. It does not touch on some areas in marriage, while others are reflected on repeatedly. It is not a handbook on marriage but rather an invitation to join in and identify yourself, and to participate in the ongoing dialogue. There is much we can learn from each other about how to live together more meaningfully.

I hope you will translate what is said here to your own relationship. If you are able to do this and can gain new insight into yourself and into the important relationship in your life, then these reflections will have achieved their purpose.

ULRICH SCHAFFER
January 1977

I have added fourteen pages of text and many new faces for this new edition of *a growing love*. A number of the photographs show people in their thirties, forties, and fifties to indicate that this book is not for young marrieds only. I hope that it, along with its two companion volumes, *love reaches out* and *for the love of children*, will find many more readers, both young and old, in years to come.

ULRICH SCHAFFER
January 1980

the dialogue of joy and pain

fused together by pain

i hurt
   when you reject me
you cry
   when you don't understand me
i give up
   when you put me down
you become frightened
   when i don't talk
i feel inadequate
   in the light of your expectations
you feel hopeless
   when nothing seems to change
i feel maimed
   when you don't answer
you are alarmed
   at my indifference
i am offended
   by your stubbornness
you are lost
   when i am so determined
i wound you
   when i feel left out of your life
you injure me
   in finding yourself

we are fused together by pain
inseparable and separate
alone and together
dependent and independent
our relationship is filled
with the paradox of living

we don't even have to talk about
right and wrong
but only focus on the growth in the pain

growth is the only alternative
to a life of creeping death
that leaves us inactive and indifferent

to us
who love God
all things have meaning
and loving God makes all things
participate in
our growth

getting my bearings

if i knew more
i could tell you more
but i am not always
in touch with myself

therefore wait
until i get my bearings
even if all i can tell you is
that i am still lost

but please allow me
to be lost

do not force me
to be strong
to be what i am not
to do what i can't do
to say what i don't mean
and to go where nothing draws me

when you allow me
to be weak with you
i feel my love growing
and i move so close to you
in the trust that grows with the love

my wish to please you

i am very glad that you love me
and also glad that you tell me so
but please don't wait for me to return
    the same statement to you

some other time i will say it
and say it before you think of it

but now i don't want to react
to feel obligated to say "and i love you too"

i have to know what i feel
without any prompting
without anyone giving me cues
because quite often my wish to please you
and to be pleased in return
gets in the way of my love for you

recognition

your eyes are receptive
to what i am saying
i can see that you are following my words
and going beyond them

and together we push forward
into new ideas
    thinking what we have never thought before
together we can experience
the ever greater joy
of living in a fascinating world

we are not separated but one
our lives touch in so many points
and i can see you
like i have never seen you before

and it dawns on me
that our relationship is a miracle
that it is the love of God emerging
in a fallen world

we are rich beyond measure
to have each other
and to grow into the likeness of God
together

decision to marry

i found the decision to marry you
very difficult
i had visions of losing my freedom
of being bound
and not being able to do the things
i had been doing up to then

i pictured myself as another nonperson
a gray blob in a gray mass
just another average guy
i was afraid of not being able to fulfill
    some of my hidden dreams

and i was afraid of your expectations
your projections and wishes
and sometimes i felt that you could only love me
    because you did not know me yet

and then i was afraid
of making the wrong choice
because i did not really know what i wanted
and whom i really wanted
and what to hope for in that person
i was afraid of the impossibility of backtracking
the one-way street of marriage

all these fears made me so irritable
so unsure and defensive
and i am grateful for your patience
for your understanding of my confusion

and now in retrospect
i know that all my fears were legitimate fears
and real threats to people who marry
because all around me i can see
    the casualties of marriage
but i am also learning that those threats
    are the fears and threats of life
    that can come true
    whether i marry or stay single
and that they *will* come true
    if i let them
if i make the choice
    to give up my dreams
if i allow my originality to dry up
if i consent to be run by my feelings

if i do not accept fully
the privilege to make decisions

waking up beside you

i wake up beside you
   as you toss and turn
   pursued by a bad dream
   by the weight of life
and i notice how much older you are

i can tell time in your face
and i become aware
that my face tells the same story
that we have passed through years
which we can never retrieve

here we are
tied to a rolling wheel
measuring out these seconds and minutes
and all the tomorrows
tumbling toward an inevitable end

looking at you on your pillow
i have to take stock
and consider what has kept us together

not money
not beauty
not compatibility
not the fear of being alone
not the hope of never getting old

but the commitment
made without guilt
without obligation or pressure
without the attempt to save or salvage

a commitment made in hope
hope in the changing person
developing in all of us

hope not fed by your good actions
hope not in myself
nor in the power of reconciliation
but hope in the earnest desire to grow
to experience the wealth
found in the unpredictability of life

hope
instilled and nurtured in us
by the spirit of God

taking my pressure off

how liberating it is to me
to just let you be
to . . . . just . . . . let . . . . you . . . . be

to know
that i am not responsible for you
that you must make your own peace with God
you must make your own decisions
you must be your own person

i am here if you want me
and only if you want me
i will not force myself on you
i will not force my ideas on you
not even if i consider them more valid

i will rest and not pressure you
and in that way give you room to change
if you wish

wait a minute

can't we stop for a minute
because we are both down
both disturbed and in agony?
can't we let everything stand
the way it is at the moment
even all the unclarity between us?

i feel that we are reaching the breaking point
and just another small load
can push us over the edge
into actions and words
which neither of us mean
    and yet they will weigh us down
    for weeks to come

when i am hurt
i cannot distinguish between
what i really mean
and what i say and do
to "get back at you"

do you know
that i really love you
in spite of how i might act?

running smoothly

it has become so quiet between us
as we pursue our duties
and live up to expectations

and i am becoming afraid of this quiet
because i know that there are things
   to be worked out
   which we are not even attempting to tackle

everything is running too smoothly
and perhaps we are engaged in a very quiet kind
   of compromise of ourselves
which will take its toll in our marriage
   later on

lack of conflict is often the best sign
of the fear of realizing what is and what isn't
and also a sign of the creeping process
   of compromise
   which brings in its wake:
   resentment frustration and often a blowup
   which can end all

let's wake up
to the riches of love
to the excitement and joy
that our relationship holds in store for us

to "know" you

and adam knew eve
and she conceived and bore cain
—genesis

because you have invited me into your life
and made yourself ready to receive me
i have been trying to come to know you
working to come close to you
to enter the hidden recesses of your mind
to understand what moves you
to know what causes your fear
to agonize through the twistings
    and turnings of your mind
to suffer your turmoil
to be abandoned with you
to be elated with you
to deny you my sentimental love
    as an act of love
to awaken you to the abyss in you
    called security
    which tells you to give up the search
to see you in all your nakedness
    without masks
to experience with you
    the fall and the resurrection

and i have made myself known to you
i have disclosed myself
    to the point of embarassment
i have allowed you to see my confusion

i have shared with you my yearning
   so unattainable
   so unrealistic
you have seen me with clenched fists
   with tears
   in a daze of unbelief
   and beside myself with joy
and you have lived that way with me
you gave and received
and together
we have dreamt laughed and suffered

and now
as a sign of our mutual knowing
   in full respect of what is yet to be known
as a manifestation of that which is
   and in anticipation of what will be
we can let our bodies melt into each other
and obliterate for moments the gulf
   that separates us
in our imperfection

and in knowing and being known
in the interaction and intertwining
   of our lives
we will bring about new life
and carry in us
the fruit of the union of body mind and spirit

please stay away

please stay away
stay back
with your kindness
with your tenderness
with your questions and answers
just give me the private space i need
to collect myself
to listen into me
and to find out how i see you

please respect my privacy
in which i must find out
who you are inside of my life
and what i think and feel about you
because now i am lost inside myself

please don't crowd me
like you have been doing
don't stand so close to me
because when you do
    i move away
    from the center of my being
    and become confused
    about us

you are preaching again

when you make statements
    that you don't even question
when you just tell me how it is
and when you pretend it to be the objective truth
    and not just your feeling
    or your understanding of the situation
then the pressure is on

then i don't know what to do
then i am trapped
    hopelessly trapped
and all my energies are devoted
to getting out of that trap

and so i don't even really react
    to what you say
but only to your trapping me
and i become unreasonable and silly
while you become more secure in what you said

please don't trap me
leave me the room to decide
and be happy
    even if i decide against your opinion
because i have to find my own way
only then can i truly come to you

let us wear three rings

the first one shall be made of metal
it is to surround us fully
and is to be shiny and clear
like a mirror
and be called love

and the second one
shall be called death
and it is to throw its circumference
around our hands and feet
so that we will work with it

and the third one shall be God
and he is not to be above us
but in and under us
so that we can stand on him
in the threat of the grayness around us

the ring around all rings
in all rings

tiredness

with fear
i realize once again
tiredness taking hold of me

i do not have enough energy
to forgive again
to begin anew
to let the past be the past

life rushes past without my involvement
you rush past
    without giving rise to an emotion in me

now
with my last bit of energy
i make contact with you
and in spite of my indifference toward you
i can feel life growing out of that contact
and my weakness is once again overcome
by confronting that
    which at first made me tired and afraid

and slowly joy is born
out of the weakness and pain

escaping from you

many times life has offered me
the chance to escape from you
not to run away with someone else
but just to withdraw imperceptibly
to become involved with my job
with my children
with books or trips
with digressions of many kinds
all at the expense of my involvement with you

perhaps i found it too strenuous
    to communicate with you
or i feared for my own sanity
    if i became more deeply involved
    with your ideas
or i found that i didn't get through to you

then came the temptation to escape from you
to take the easier way out
to be less involved with you
to spend less time
to tune out when you talked
to say: i am tired
        i have a hard time listening
        i don't understand (often meaning that
        i don't want to understand)
to slowly divorce my inner person from you

and because it begins so subtly
we would not notice the beginning cold
between us
but our marriage would start its slow decline
its gradual dissolution
and the eventual destruction
would be complete
if neither of us would notice
that anything was wrong

oneness and uniqueness

many times i have felt
that a good talk
words spoken in greater love
   filled with more seriousness
   more carefully chosen
   and more sensitively delivered
that those words would make the difference

but deep down i know
that words do not make the difference
that we are separated by our uniqueness
that we are two adults in search of ourselves
   in search of our lives and meanings
   and that we will inevitably clash
   if we don't compromise ourselves
   if we don't buckle under
   and become accommodating for the sake of peace

and therefore i will take those differences
as signs of our maturation
as signs of our uniqueness
and will not constantly attempt
   to reduce those differences
   in order to create a oneness
   that is simply uniformity

the oneness of which Jesus talks
must come from him
and not from our feeble efforts
to deny who we are
for the sake of a false unity

suggestions

i have so many suggestions for you
how you can change
what you should or could do
how you can tackle a specific problem

i have suggestions for change
so that you can get along with me better
i have suggestions which will bring you closer to me

but you won't listen

and then i hear your suggestions for me
how i can change
what i should and could do
how i could tackle certain problems
how i can get along with you better

now we have decided not to heed
     each other's suggestions
and there we are!

maybe
just maybe
we could try telling *ourselves only*
but i won't even say that to you
i will only say:
here is what i can do:

i must realize
that ultimately
all your decisions are out of my hands

alone together

alone together

to realize that we are both alone
that we are born alone
and that we will die alone
that we must decide alone
and that we have to stand alone before God
that no one can take any important step
for us
that realization sets us free

suddenly we have nothing to lose
and we can embark on the adventure
of finding community
of finding and sharing love

then let's take our findings
as a miracle in this cold world
and not as something to be expected
as a gift and not as a right
as grace and not as justice

different ways out

on days when i don't feel anything for you
when i think that i could live just as well
without you
i ask myself
if my love is dead
if it has stopped being
after years of hard work on our relationship

i don't like to pursue this question
because i am afraid
of certain answers
but the question won't go away
it keeps coming back
and i have to face it
sooner or later

at first i take the well-known way out:
i try to convince myself that i love you
that you are important to me
i recall all the good times
all our sharing
i picture the many positive experiences
i paint pictures in bright colors
i block out what i feel right now
i warm up old feelings
but all that won't last
my fear will come back
twice as strong

then i take the second way out:
i compare our marriage with others
especially those that seem to be worse marriages
hopeless ones
and i feel a little better
take heart and want to try again
but that does not seem to be enough either
because i know
that i have to live *my* marriage
i have to find the way to *you*
and that is so difficult

when i am totally exhausted
and think that i can't go on anymore
a third way out offers itself:
we should separate
because we just won't make it together
and in order to go this way
i have to find fault
and usually find it with you
then freedom seems to beckon (i hope)
everything will be different (i tell myself)
then i will find myself (i promise myself)

three ways
three ways out
three possibilities of not having to meet
     the situation
three impossibilities

then i realize
that at this point of bankruptcy
the miracle is to take place
here is the chance for love in conjunction with faith
to grow beyond just good feelings
for each other

this is the desert
the place without water
this is the fallen nature of man
here we are
this is our inadequacy
our sin
our lack of power over ourselves
our inability to help ourselves

but
this is also the starting point of grace
the test of faith
the place God wanted to have us
    in order to talk to us
here our only hope lies in trusting God
    because we have failed
here is the place of transformation
    not overnight
    but in a slow and steady building
this is the time of praying and screaming
    in truth without deception

what has broken apart
can be joined again

heavy silence

we are separated by a heavy silence
and we don't seem to get on top of that
we can't overcome ourselves
and we begin to brood
and to weigh each other down
with negative thoughts
with bad vibrations

i will break out
and make the first move
say the first word
to open up the discussion again

i hope for your response
and even if it does not come
i will continue to remain open
ready for your participation
but without any coercion on my part

rights

you are not mine
and i am not yours

your time is not mine
and my time is not yours
to be wasted

my ideas
do not necessarily
have to become your ideas as well
and i feel no obligation to adopt your views

i have no rights
and no right to expect anything from you
because your life is a gift to me
and my life and being is a gift to you
which i can choose to give or to withhold

but i am glad to hear your ideas
and perhaps to change mine accordingly
and i am happy to share with you
what moves and shapes me

i enjoy giving my time to you
and your time with me
shall be worthwhile

i have given myself to you
and i am receiving you

we are married
as though we weren't
as though we were
as though we weren't

talking it out or not

there always seem to be things
that i can't say
because i must take into account
whether our relationship is ready

i hope that i am not rationalizing
    any hidden fears
and i hope that i can talk in such a way
    that you will understand
    even if you don't agree

i am also learning
that some things need not be said
if they are worked through in me
if i learn to love questions fears and doubts
if i accept them as an integral part of life

then that secret inside of me
    will not poison me but make me richer
it will not eat out my insides
    but make me stronger
i will not hold it over you as a threat
    but i will enjoy my correct timing
    when i come out with it

i am realizing
how important timing is in a marriage

spiral

your freedom
is always tied in with mine

i can let you go free fully
if i am being let go by you

my freedom liberates you
which liberates me
which liberates you
etc.
etc.
etc.

it can be an upward
or a downward spiral

i can choose
you can choose
we can choose

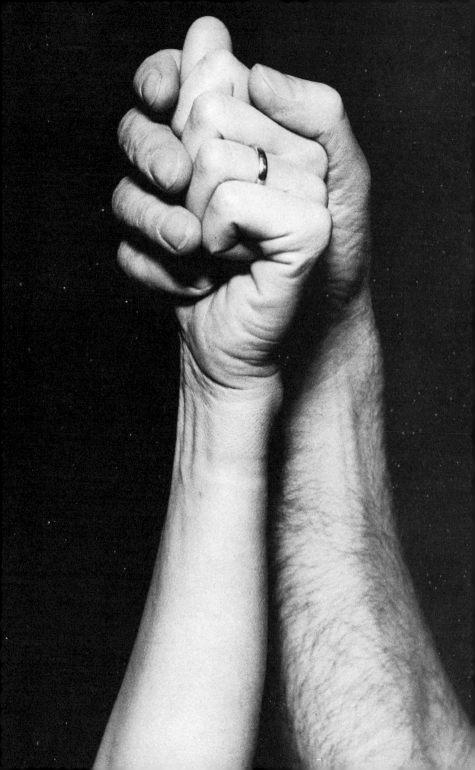

more room to grow

just give me room
more room to grow
when everyone else is closing in on me
and the world seems like a cage

just give me room
more room to grow
when the world around me
asks me to remain unchanged

just give me room
more room to grow
released from the image
you have of me

just give me room
more room to grow
toward the likeness
that lies buried in me

in the silence of this night

now
in the middle of night
alone with my thoughts
my life clearly spread out in front of me
a heavy sadness overcomes me
and i become conscious
of the insurmountable distance
between all people
including you and me
all the things we share
are not protection against this awareness

and yet it is not unbearable
because sometimes i sense what it will be like
when we will be complete and perfect
then i get a glimpse of the wholeness
and an insight into the secret of the overall plan

we are wanderers in the loneliness of this night
and perhaps we are more united
   by the knowledge of this loneliness
   by the suffering under our incompleteness
   by the yearning for fulfillment
than by any attempt to pretend that it isn't so

i love you
and reach out to you
sometimes our fingertips touch
and we are witnesses of the miracle

as i move away from you

as i begin to be more self-sufficient
as i become more independent of you
as i begin not to "need" you
as i begin to accept my loneliness
    and explore it
as i begin to live without expectations of you
as i refuse to live up
    to your expectations of me
as i lose the need to react
    because i am finding my identity
as i delve into my own depths
    unaccompanied by you

and as you do the same

the miracle takes place:
you come closer
we learn from each other
we share
we fulfill expectations
we create a pull
because now the confines are gone
now we are no longer shackled to each other
we are no longer bound and tied by our "love"
we are free
we are in love
a renewed love
we are a gift to each other
unexpected and surprising
far beyond our hope

letting go

letting you go free
into making all the mistakes
   you want to make
into rejecting me
into finding new values
into changing your mind
   just when i have understood you
into not caring at all
into caring too much
into an unprotected life
into a lonely existence
that is what i have to learn

i have to learn
to let you go
so simple
and yet so difficult

demands

i make demands on you
but i don't state them openly
i just expect you to pick up on them
and when you don't
i get angry that you can be so insensitive

indignation anger and resentment grow in me
i become upset
try to hold it in
until i finally can't anymore
and explode

and you say:
i didn't know that you expected all that from me
why didn't you say something
i would have gladly done some of those things for you
i just didn't notice

but i am too upset
and your words sound like an excuse
i stay with my feelings of resentment
i savor my anger
to make my blow-up worthwhile

and it doesn't take long
until you too
can only defend yourself
and inconsequential things become big issues

if i had stated my expectations and hopes openly
when it all started
this would not have happened

the how-could-you game

how could you say that?
how could you do that?
you can't mean that?

all the questions i am asking
are really not questions
but my way of accusing you
of not loving me

with every question i ask
in that tone of voice
i am also saying
that i would never do or say that
and i can't imagine
that you could act like that
if you really loved me

i am limiting your expression
i am putting guilt on you
i am asking for evidence of your love
and i am dictating
what that evidence should be

forgive me for being so calculating
and manipulative
i do not want to force a show of your love

yearning

she yearns for a fuller life
wants to live with greater intensity
but he finds it "not necessary"
even when admitting
that "she needs something like that"

he gives her the freedom
and she soon finds others
(often women living in similar marriages)
or she reads books that help her
but she does it with a guilty conscience
because she notices
how she slowly moves away from her husband
yet her yearning is too strong
just to be put aside

they drift apart
and soon they no longer talk
    about what concerns them
they build separate lives
separate worlds

and yet she wishes nothing more than to share
her searching and finding and searching
with her husband
to discover life together
to grow towards each other
but he does not see her need
and the loneliness
into which they are both
falling

what's really happening?

learning to know what you really mean

when you say
CAN'T YOU DO THAT FOR ONCE?
you might actually mean:
—i am tired of your irresponsibility
—i resent telling you things
—i don't like myself for having to remind you

when you say
YOU DON'T REALLY CARE THAT MUCH, DO YOU?
you might actually mean:
—it hurts me that you care so little
—please care more!
—it hurts me that we communicate like strangers
—i am waiting for you to woo me again
   to love me
   for me to be special to you

when you say
I AM SO TIRED OF LIFE!
you might actually mean:
—our life has lost its real intensity
—please do something!
—we have become what we did not want to become
—i don't want to try to convince you anymore
   that our life centers too much around working eating
   and tv

when you say
I CAN'T STAND YOU WHEN YOU'RE LIKE THAT!
you might actually mean:
—i feel threatened by you

—can't you see that i lack all self-respect
  and all sense of self-worth
—i just don't know how to answer you
—i don't like myself when you bring the worst
  out in me
—please don't play that role
  because i can see right through it

when you say
YOU ALWAYS/NEVER DO THAT!
you might actually mean:
—i am frustrated that neither of us
  can really listen to the other
—your coolness bothers me
—please react
  i am as aggressive as i can be
—i feel ignored and want to communicate with you

i know that we use words to hide, to hit
to run away
words are smoke screens and security builders
words are bait to be swallowed
  by the unsuspecting
words are arm-twisters and weakening agents
words are shots barbs and hooks
words are mirrors of the soul
words are cries for help
words are words and so much more

because i want to know you
and to communicate with you
i will be open to what lies behind your words

if only . . .

if only i could say
   what is really inside of me
if only you could convey to me
   the images and pictures that rest in you
   and contribute to your life
if only i could feel
   what you are going through now
if only you could see
   what is invisible but real to me
if only i could
   live through your past with you
if only you could
   decode my gestures
if only i could interpret better
   the many faces you wear
if only you could hear
   with your heart
   what i am saying with my heart
if only i could
   get into your inner space
   and you could get into mine
then communication would be so much easier

but i know
that eyes ears minds and hearts
can learn
to take in the world
much more fully through faith

i *will* move closer to you
my love

making choices

he complains about being
bound
trapped
depressed
manipulated
pressured
by the world around him

he is bound by her statements
   because he is allowing himself to be bound
he is trapped by her actions
   because he is allowing himself to be trapped
he is depressed
   because he can then put the blame on her
he is manipulated
   because he refuses to make his own choices
he is pressured
   because he is not willing
   to face the consequences
   of doing what others might not like

he is looking for causes outside of himself
he wants to place the blame somewhere else
so he won't have to change
he is not accepting responsibility
   for his decisions
and therefore he is not free
and is a puppet to all those
   who care to pull his string

he has to learn the difference between
   feeling bound and being bound
   feeling trapped and being trapped
between feeling depressed
   and acting out of that depression
between not exercising his choices
   and being given no choices
between being pressured
   or just afraid to live
   according to his convictions

he has to look inside of himself
   to become free
and to meet the giver of limitless freedom

the work of love

we have been told
   that love overwhelms us
we have been shown in films
   that people fall in love in an instant
we have read
   that yet others simply could not help themselves
   and had to become unfaithful to their partners
we have heard the champions of free love declare
   that monogamy is unnatural
we have been brainwashed to believe
   that love depends on our good looks
   and driving the right car
we have been told
   that love comes
   and goes

but very few have talked to us about
the *work* of love
about the *energy* expended to forgive
about the *strain* to survive the daily grind
   with a heart still capable of loving
about the *task* of self-sacrifice
   without dying in the process
about the use of the *will*
   against the weakness of our emotions

the work of love
the energy to love
the decision to continue loving
in the hope of being transformed beyond ourselves

the approval game

almost every day i have to learn
that the approval you can give me
   can never take the place of self-approval
that my feelings of inadequacy
   can not be dealt with
   by your kind words
that the guilt which i carry
   will not be alleviated
   by your verbal support of me

to seek my security in you
and to determine my identity and worth
by your approval
is to make myself an extension of you
thereby degrading both you and myself
and degrading our relationship
because we become things
owning and being owned
rather than people
in charge of their own decisions

i then make you responsible
   for something that only i can do
i weigh you down
   with my guilt and feelings of inadequacy
   so i won't have to bear them

i have to search in myself
    for the value of my actions
    of my being
and i must turn to God
and realize that my value
is that of being a child of God
guiltless
more than merely adequate
and fully approved
the way i am

how easy it is
to find someone who will be approving of me
who will like what i do
and find pleasant what i say
    at least for a while
but ultimately that approval
    will also not be enough
and a void will remain in me
    until i find my real worth
and the source of my being

a difficult sign of love

i did not understand
that your strong reactions to me
    had nothing to do with me
but were your way of freeing yourself
    from the world crowding in on you
    trying to kill the essential you
    the being in us which must not be destroyed
    if we are to go on living in an alive way

i am closest to you
    and you naturally hit out at me
used me as your scapegoat
and i in my immaturity reacted
    by hitting back
    by blaming you
    by making you my scapegoat

the difference was:
you were fighting for your life
    while i was only reacting
you were fighting for your identity
    while i was only fighting to maintain my honor
    my sense of being right

i will now take it as a sign of love
    when you lash out at me
    when you kick to remain free
i know that you must trust me enough
    to choose me as the person
    through whom you want to grow

caricatures of marriage

1

their marriage began with their bodies
and never moved beyond them
and now
they indulge in legalized prostitution

2

he is embarrassed because
she does not understand quickly enough
she is embarrassed because
she does not measure up

both are concerned about covering up
about appearing together
about projecting a good wholesome image
and neither
is really concerned about the other
for the other's sake

3

when they married
there was love
but soon their respective families
(which felt that they must also
marry each other)
smothered that love

now the two married people
communicate as extensions of their families
with each other

4

the focus of their marriage
was their child
to whom their love flowed
and stopped
(what kind of love was this?)

both felt fulfilled
and no need to communicate with each other
until their child could make decisions
and would decide for one
and against the other

then communication started
but only over who would have possession
of the child
until
the child
was torn
apart

5

in public
their marriage was a put-down game
which both played expertly
for the amusement of others

now they play the same game
in private

staying together for the children

sometimes we choose reasons for our actions
    to avoid choosing other reasons
and often we prefer the second-best reasons
    over the truly best
because the truly best
    are too strenuous and costly

and so people stay together
because of children or for economic reasons
because of the position they hold in society
because they are so accustomed to each other
because of fear of loneliness
because of what others will say

but they don't realize
that they are not staying *together*
they are just *staying* together

they are just using the same house
the same car and bank
and the same children

perhaps the time has come to decide
to stay together by making a new commitment
or to break apart
perhaps to make visible the alienation
    that has been growing for so long

once again
to honor the integrity and honesty
of each other

sex experts

there are the technicians of love
who see in love an act
who "make" love like a product
who talk about technique and style
who have statistics to back up their statements
who time orgasms
who talk about constants and coefficients
who have many suggestions for revitalization
   for weary travelers on this road

then there are the analysts of love
who think they are taking love
   to a higher plane than the technicians
by talking about motives
traumas and complexes
dependencies and expectations
and they turn out to be technicians as well
technicians in a different field
manipulators of the soul
calculators of feeling
engineers of the unconscious
but equally devoid of the breath
which brings new life

and then there are those who care to know
who go beyond technique and style
beyond mood and feeling
who center their sex in their love
and their love in the will to know
   and to be known
   to unfold and enlarge
and to be reborn with and in each other

forgive me

forgive me
where i used you
to satisfy myself
where i didn't regard your feelings enough

forgive my shortsightedness
and my lack of self-discipline

i don't want to feel cheap now
i still want to be allowed to come close to you
to build up what my selfishness destroys

please don't shut me out of your life
but teach me love and respect
and the interconnectedness of body soul and spirit

i want to understand better
that nothing can be excluded
that all levels of our being must be incorporated
if we truly want to meet
so that the meeting of our bodies
constitutes the same praise
that we experience in our spirit

hiding from each other

they are both afraid
although at first glance
they seem secure and together

they are both afraid to confront
to meet head-on
to say clearly and unmistakably
    where they are at
to put their finger on the wound
to show their need

all their energies are devoted
to hiding from each other
and to pretending that they are not hiding

while inside them
the wasteland is slowly spreading
leaving behind it the desolate landscape of fear

and fear
like a cancer grows in secret

all for God

he has decided
to be totally available for God
to serve him
to listen only to him
and he feels good about this decision

but he seems to have forgotten
that life continues
that he has a family
for which he is responsible
that his children wait for him to have time
and that his wife wants to live in partnership with him

he talks a lot about God
goes to committee meetings and planning discussions
he preaches and counsels
he throws himself more and more
into the work of the kingdom of God
he is a sought-after speaker
some can't do without him
truly a man after the heart of God

at home a woman sits alone
and children grow up without a father
because even if he is at home
he is not really at home

this marriage and family
(even though they seem to function well)
are breaking up
are broken
because a man is doing
what God never expected of him

different perspectives

she:
you leave the house in the morning
meet people
and have a job that you enjoy

he:
you can stay home
pursue the thoughts that you started
determine the course of your day

she:
your life is rich in experiences
you encounter yourself differently
in the various situations of the day

he:
you don't have to adapt to situations or people
you can even be absentminded
because no one expects anything from you

she:
i stay at home
cook sew and clean up
where i just finished cleaning up
my life is the same every day

he:
i have to be awake and aware
and confronted with new situations
i have to make decisions constantly
and that is draining

she:
i am cut off
alone with my thoughts
i cannot try them on anyone
i am caught up in myself
and feel like i'm locked in

he:
i have to leave my real self at home
and talk about unimportant matters
as though they were important
i have to listen to stupid jokes
and i am expected to laugh

she:
when you come home
i would like to know what has happened to you
throughout your day
i want to share in the movement
of your life

he:
when i come home
i want to leave my workday far behind me
i want to relax

she:
then i want to go out with you
to experience something together

he:
then i want to have a quiet evening at home
together with you

both:
it helps me
to see your point of view
to see that what i yearn for
is sometimes hard for you
and i notice how important it is
that we share openly how we feel
because life is difficult and easy
for both of us
and we need each other
to create a balance

being all to each other

he seems almost obsessed with the idea
that *she* must be everything to him
that *she* must give him confirmation
   for his actions
   even if she does not understand them
that *she* must understand all his emotional needs
that *she* must be his equal in mental ability
that *she* must understand his music
that *she* must care for poetry

and she in turn feels
that everything that bothers her
must be answered by *him*
that *he* must be as interested in films
   as she is
that *he* must be the person to go to
   for understanding in every area of her life

and with these assumptions
they both do everything together
they spend much time trying to keep up
   with each other
because they are afraid
   of hurting their relationship
   by letting someone else in
they dare not think their thoughts to the end
they dare not allow themselves to feel
   what they feel
and this causes frustration resentment
   and a feeling of being trapped in marriage

they must both realize their limitations
and understand that they need others
   to help them to grow
that there will be times
   when they will be understood better
   by a friend
and that this is no cause for jealousy
that this does not make their marriage worth less
but will simply allow the riches of others
   to flow into that marriage

such openness toward others
and the freedom to pursue things alone
will take the pressure off their marriage
and show them that they do not need to safeguard
their marriage
by trying to be all to each other
and that love can grow
in the full affirmation of our differences
and limitations

love is not the natural state

love is not the natural state
of our lives
but selfishness jealousy and indifference are

love does not come with a ceremony
nor with wishful thinking
and it cannot be forced to come by commitment

love never comes to stay
it can't be stored for the future
and past love does not answer to present needs

love is the state of having God in us
love comes as a gift
love must be renewed constantly

love grows out of our experience with God
love grows out of our acceptance of ourselves
love grows out of our acceptance of each other

a "good" marriage

they have a good marriage
and they are considered lucky by others
but both of them have the feeling
that they are both pretending

their happiness is related to a missing insight
to an unopenness and a lacking trust
their sensitivity has been dulled
   by their happiness
   which is not real happiness
and both notice that there must be more
that there must be more to life

they are surrounded by their good friends
who notice nothing
and who would be very surprised
if everything were suddenly
not to be just perfect
and who would only say:
—don't you love each other any more?
—everything was ok up to now
   what's going on?
—don't be silly!
—everything will be fine again
   just you wait and see!

these remarks may be well-meant
and even spoken with kindness
but they show little concern
for the growth of this couple

because the dimly burning wick of great yearning
    for greater fullness of God
    for deeper fellowship
    for meaningful encounters
    and for a love that can change
is snuffed out
by words spoken in careless love

everything now depends upon taking
    this growing sensitivity
    this unclear feeling
    this quiet yearning
and channeling them into paths
that will bring about the wanted change

Lord give them friends
who will not be afraid to help them honestly
friends who will not continue pretending
    with them
but who will penetrate deeply
into the secrets of fellowship with them

be close to them
with your comforting hand
in this time of renewal
with its joy and pain

anger talks

1
my anger is my way of saying
that i want you to see my worth
it is a frustrated effort
    not well articulated
that i am valuable
that i should be valuable to you

with my anger i am trying to make you
    take a stand
    make some kind of commitment
with my anger i want to force you to act

2
with my anger i want to tell you
that it is not enough
what is happening between us
that i am not satisfied with our relationship
that i am looking for more
and that i am desperate in my search

3
with my anger
i have a way of externalizing
what is chewing me up inside

i can get my hands on my half-baked ideas
on my feelings that can't yet be articulated
in my anger i can be creative

the destruction of a man
by his "christian wife"

she was told to stick with him
to "bear" him
to be strong by his side

and she stayed with him
through thick and thin
through sickness and health
through good times and bad times

she stayed with him through emotional abuse
through his temper tantrums
through his irresponsibility

she stuck by his side
she "bore" him
she remained strong in it all

she trusted God
and did it for God's sake
and for the children

she stayed with him through all that

    did she really stay *with* him?
was she at his side
and on his side
or did she just share his bed and his bank?

was her "bearing him"
(as a "good christian wife" should)
not her own twisted way of revenge

because her "holiness" was so hard for him
    to bear
and caused him to further lose faith in himself
so that finally he saw himself as only weak
while she was strong
and he resented her more and more
but could not even act on it
because she looked so right
and he looked so wrong
and of course everyone was backing her up
praising her christian virtues

perhaps an act of trust on her part
would have been
to let her temper flare
to show her own weakness
to refuse to be strong
and to be unable to bear everything

he regressed
and became less and less capable
while she became stronger and stronger
until she did not need him anymore
and could discard him
like an empty hull

both lacked the conviction
to live outwardly
what was happening in them
and both ended up playing roles
they had never wanted to play

revision

i seek shelter in our love
   and realize that it does not shelter me
i seek rest in our love
   and find fearfulness
i seek comfort in our love
   and find apprehension

and it dawns on me
that love does not always express itself
in the usual forms
that it disguises itself
becomes hard to understand
and even remains unrecognized at times
but that it is still love

love can disturb
   because it cleans up and clarifies
love can cause fear
   because growth causes pain
love can trigger uncertainty
   because our certainties
   no longer answer our questions
and where love grows
   sentimentality has to go

and i probe
whether my love is inseparably
joined to faith:
the ability to hope in the dark
to believe against the onslaught of despair
and to love without seeing

a collection of good-for-nothing looks

the don't-give-me-that-hi-stuff-you're-
    late-again look
the nice-guy-who-wouldn't-hurt-a-fly look
the wife-as-doormat look
the honey-can't-you-see-how-right-i-am look
the i-never-want-to-talk-to-you-again look
the i-never-want-to-talk-to-you-again-
    unless-you-shape-up look
the look-how-nice-i-am-i-even-forgive-you look
the you-can't-do-that-to-me look
the you-have-it-coming look
the you-can't-be-that-mean look
the you-hurt-my-feelings-again look
the you-still-think-you're-right? look
the husband-as-scapegoat look
the i-am-just-a-housewife-tied-to-kitchen look
the i've-just-caught-you-in-your-own-
    words look
the don't-you-realize-i-have-just-caught-
    you look
the you've-got-to-have-a-guilty-conscience-
    when-i-look-at-you-with-my-big-eyes look

complete the list
with your own favorite looks
and ask yourself
what you are really trying to accomplish
with those looks

have you tried words to convey
what is going on inside of you?

thank you for . . .

thank you

1
thank you for the care you take
in making out of our house a home
in creating out of our living room
more than just a good room
   but a place in which my mind can be free
can rest and be at ease

i will try never to see it as your role
but as a gift you give to me
as a surprise

2
thank you
for the flowers on my desk
for the mended sweater
for the choice of music
with which you woke me

3
thank you
for being a mirror
to me

4
thank you for your independence
which frees me to do more for you
than i could do otherwise

5

thank you for granting me silence
thank you for swallowing your words
when you noticed my inability
to deal with yet more information

6

thank you
for not judging me according to my capabilities
and for treating me as a person
rather than as a collection of roles to be exploited

7

thank you
for distinguishing
between sympathy and love

8

thank you
for your attacks
on my indifference and carelessness

9

thank you
for just taking over
when i couldn't anymore
when too much was just too much

10

thank you
for your patience
allowing me to develop at my own speed

11

thank you
for sharing your fear, your joy
your struggle, your love
and your life with me

in praise of two people

they are married
as though they weren't
because they don't possess each other
but let each other go
to develop as necessary
and yet they are committed to each other
and really care

they share their lives with each other
but don't become exclusive
and unmarried people are drawn
into their marriage
and can feel at home
and add to the marriage

they can lean on each other
    without becoming dependent in an unhealthy way
they can judge each other
    without condemning unconditionally
they can point out mistakes in each other
    but do so with a firm belief
    in the other's ability to change

they do not live as extensions of each other
they do not play roles
    to make life simpler
    or because the laws of society expect this
they have long learned to accept pain
    as an integral part of love
    and they do not run away
    if pain comes most sharply
    from the person they love the most

their love does not smother them
they are still free to disagree
free to shout
even to be disgusted with each other
without breaking up

they dare to behave that way
because there is a solidness in their love
which constitutes the basis on which they stand
so that their decision for each other
is not dependent on acts and words
but is centered in the will
to make the miracle of community come true

and yet this solidness
does not render them invulnerable
but they have learned to include
the wounds of their vulnerability
in their concept of love

they are strong in their tenderness
and tender in their strength

they are so marvelously separate
independent
alone
private
and because of that
they can be so rich in their life together

to be alive

to love you is
to remain alive
to become
to be
and to further become
as an act of love for you

and we must not ask of each other
that we diminish our lives
    to keep our love alive
because that would be the death of our love

to love you
is to add imagination to our relationship
and to focus on our wholeness
in the midst of our brokenness

to love
is to be supremely alive
and to be supremely alive
is to love

details

1
to say
"i know you"
is to kill you in me

2
marriage is
starting to love
over and over again

3
in marriage
pain has two possible consequences:
if rejected it separates
if accepted and affirmed
it brings closer together

4
love matures
as the lovability of the other
disappears

5
love sometimes shelters us
by exposing us

6

perhaps more would change
in our marriage
if i told myself
all the things i tell you

7

i must reach the point
of not blaming you nor myself anymore
and learn to forgive myself and you
because we have been forgiven

8

sometimes it seems impossible
to talk about love

perhaps then we can talk about:
commitment
responsibility
activating our will
making choices
respect
self-love
vulnerability
consequences of our actions
self-disclosure
the willingness to bear pain
acceptance

and when we have done that
we will have talked about love

love is beyond words

love cannot be forced
   but it can be yearned for
love cannot be earned
   but it can be received as a surprise
love cannot be required
   but it can be waited for
love cannot be made
   but conditions for love to grow
   can be created
love cannot be legislated
   but it can be wished for
love cannot be pushed for
   but it can be drawn out
love cannot be expected
   but it can be hoped for

love is not only:
having been faithful
doing the housework
earning the money
not leaving the partner
not shouting or being angry
buying presents
following rules

love is more than an act of the will
more than good feelings
more than taking on the challenge
   and encountering another person
love is beyond words
it is elusive and comes in many disguises
which we often only recognize in retrospect
but
love always points beyond itself
to the origin and goal of love

it is beautiful with you

your gentle hand surprises me
when suddenly it is in mine
for a moment i don't know
where i end and you begin

arm in arm we walk through the park
and watch the swan with its young
as we did years ago
and behind us
we can hear the laughter of our children

we stroll along *our* shopping street
content not to buy anything
because we don't need anything
we are rich in not having any wishes
at least not today

i call you to watch the sunset with me
it is almost unreal
and no one would believe us
if we painted it in those colors

i watch you reading a book
and fall in love all over again
with the stranger sitting opposite me
you look up
because you have sensed me looking

i call you on the telephone
and you answer as though i were a stranger
for a moment i can be that stranger
i can change my voice
and fool you for a second
but then you recognize me
and i say:
no
i didn't want anything
just wanted to let you know what i was doing
no i have no questions
just wanted to hear your voice
that's all

we eat together
and delay the end of the meal
because the food is so good
and because the end is an end
behind which we can never go back

going swimming
we change in front of each other
and even now
after years
i am still struck by the fact
that it is all right to see you naked
and for you to see me

we can hear our children in the next room
only their voices
without being able to understand their words
and we are overcome by a feeling of joy
which would be unbearable
     if it were any stronger
our lives are opened up in a new way
through our children
as we experience their surprises of living
and we see ourselves in a new light
not only as father and mother

we sit across from each other
look up at the same time
and the inexplicable happens
the eye-in-eye
the indescribable
the heart-in-heart
and for an instant
we are lost in each other
and when we come to again
and return to this world
we are one

in search of love

1

sometimes we search for love
in the mystical and mysterious aspects of life
and don't realize
that we are already moving away from love

we don't realize that the mystical
comes disguised in everydayness:
in bread on the table
in the opening and closing of my hand
in the glance i register

that is the transforming presence
of the love of God

2

sometimes we search for love
in the external and tangible
and don't realize
that we are already moving away from love

we don't realize
that the visible world
is only the loose covering of truth
waiting to enter our lives
through the silent doors
of our hearts

3

approaching the world
with a heart being transformed by God
brightened by grace
enlightened by the perspective of suffering
will reduce all the phenomena of the world
to one: the presence of God
in the inner and outer world
and ultimately the realization
that the inner and outer world
match perfectly in every detail

that is the beginning of fusion with God
the ultimate reentry into our origin
living and being from-and-towards-him

4

then love will be inseparable from God
and the knowledge of God
will be the understanding of love

about the author

Ulrich Schaffer was born in Germany in 1942. At the age of ten he and his family moved to Canada, where he has lived since. He writes in both English and German and has published eight books of poetry and meditations in Germany. His first major English publication was *love reaches out*. *A growing love* can be considered a continuation of the first book.

Ulrich teaches European literature at Douglas College in New Westminister, British Columbia. He and his wife Traudi have two daughters.

Ulrich Schaffer
7320 Ridge Dr.
Burnaby, British Columbia
Canada

Cover photo: U. Schaffer
The photo of Ulrich and Traudi Schaffer on the facing page was taken by John Wiebe